PIANO • VOCAL • GUITAR

BROADWAY
SHEET MUSIC COLLECTION
2010–2017

D1599653

ISBN 978-1-5400-0418-5

HAL•LEONARD®

7777 W. BLUEMOUND RD. P.O. BOX 13819 MILWAUKEE, WI 53213

Visit Hal Leonard Online at
www.halleonard.com

CONTENTS

ANYWHERE BUT HERE
from HONEYMOON IN VEGAS

Music and Lyrics by
JASON ROBERT BROWN

BEAUTIFUL CITY
from GODSPELL

Music and Lyrics by
STEPHEN SCHWARTZ

BOULEVARD OF BROKEN DREAMS

featured in AMERICAN IDIOT

Words by BILLIE JOE
Music by GREEN DAY

I walk a lone-ly road, the on-ly one that I ___ have ev-er known.
I'm walk-ing down the line that di-vides me ___ some-where in my

Don't know where it goes, but it's home to me ___ and I walk a-lone. ___
mind. On the bor-der-line of the edge and ___ where I walk a-lone. ___

18

DUST AND ASHES
from NATASHA, PIERRE & THE GREAT COMET OF 1812

Music and Lyrics by
DAVE MALLOY
Based on *War and Peace* by Leo Tolstoy

30

EVERLASTING
from TUCK EVERLASTING

Music by CHRIS MILLER
Lyrics by NATHAN TYSEN

37

FLY, FLY AWAY

from CATCH ME IF YOU CAN

Lyrics by SCOTT WITTMAN
and MARC SHAIMAN
Music by MARC SHAIMAN

FALLING SLOWLY
from the Broadway Musical ONCE

Words and Music by GLEN HANSARD
and MARKETA IRGLOVA

now you're gone. ___

FIGHT THE DRAGONS

from BIG FISH

Music and Lyrics by
ANDREW LIPPA

FOOLISH TO THINK
from A GENTLEMAN'S GUIDE TO LOVE & MURDER

Music by STEVEN LUTVAK
Lyrics by ROBERT L. FREEDMAN
and STEVEN LUTVAK

MONTY: Fool-ish to think she would mar-ry you. Why would she sink so low? You've on-ly a claim to a no-ble old name.

who could de - ny now and then pigs can fly? _____

Tempo I

Who will look fool - ish then? _____

Who will look fool - ish

a tempo

then? _____

HOME
from the Broadway Musical WONDERLAND

Music by FRANK WILDHORN
Lyrics by JACK MURPHY

I BELIEVE

from the Broadway Musical THE BOOK OF MORMON

Words and Music by TREY PARKER
ROBERT LOPEZ and MATT STONE

THE LIFE THAT YOU WISHED FOR

from CHAPLIN

Words and Music by
CHRISTOPHER CURTIS

IN LOVE WITH YOU

from the Musical FIRST DATE

Music and Lyrics by ALAN ZACHARY
and MICHAEL WEINER

100

You al - ways crit - i - cized __ the clothes that I ____ would wear __

and found a way __ of point - ing out ____ my thin - ning hair. __ Real - ly nice!

You turned me veg - an, which I to - tal - ly ____ de - spise, ____ and I'm

pret - ty sure you laughed __ that time I said, "Let's com - pro - mise!" ____

IT ALL FADES AWAY

from THE BRIDGES OF MADISON COUNTY

Music and Lyrics by
JASON ROBERT BROWN

Freely

a cappella   N.C.

There was some-thing in a des - ert.___ There was some-place wild and green, And a

child ___ in a vil-lage I ___ passed through. There are plac-es that I've trav-eled, ___ And so

man - y things ___ I've seen, And ___ it all fades a - way ___ but

113

IT MUST BE BELIEVED TO BE SEEN

from CHARLIE AND THE CHOCOLATE FACTORY

Music by MARC SHAIMAN
Lyrics by SCOTT WITTMAN
and MARC SHAIMAN

Misterioso e più mosso (straight 8ths)

JOURNEY TO THE PAST

from the Broadway Musical ANASTASIA

Words and Music by LYNN AHRENS
and STEPHEN FLAHERTY

ME AND THE SKY

from COME FROM AWAY

Music and Lyrics by IRENE SANKOFF
and DAVID HEIN

MODEL BEHAVIOR
from WOMEN ON THE VERGE OF A NERVOUS BREAKDOWN

Words and Music by
DAVID YAZBEK

What was the name of that cheese that I like?

IVAN: *Pepa, Pepa sweetheart. Listen, I need to tell you …*
MECHANICAL VOICE: *Tape is full. End of messages.*

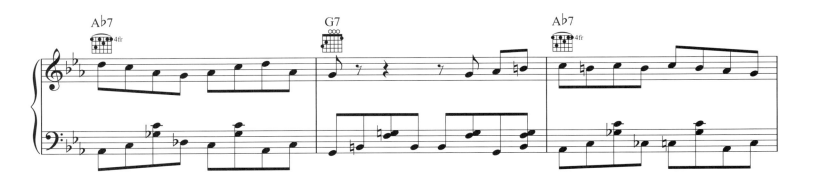

Pe - pa, o - kay now e - ven your ma-chine's ig - nor - ing me. _____

156

MY GIRL

featured in MOTOWN: THE MUSICAL

Words and Music by SMOKEY ROBINSON
and RONALD WHITE

Moderately

hon - ey, the bees __ en - vy me.

I've got a ____ sweet - er song ____

than the birds in the trees.

D.S. al Coda

Well, _

CODA

(My girl.) Ooh, ____ hoo. ____

ON MY WAY

from VIOLET

Music by JEANINE TESORI
Lyrics by BRIAN CRAWLEY

Look at her skin, Chi - na white, tis - sue thin. Look how the light cuts clear ___ to the bone, gives her skin ___ such a tone. I'd take it

170

ONE OF THE GREAT ONES

from the Broadway Musical A BRONX TALE

Music by ALAN MENKEN
Lyrics by GLENN SLATER

180

ONE PERFECT MOMENT

from BRING IT ON

Music by TOM KITT
Lyrics by AMANDA GREEN
and LIN-MANUEL MIRANDA

Freely, with slight urgency

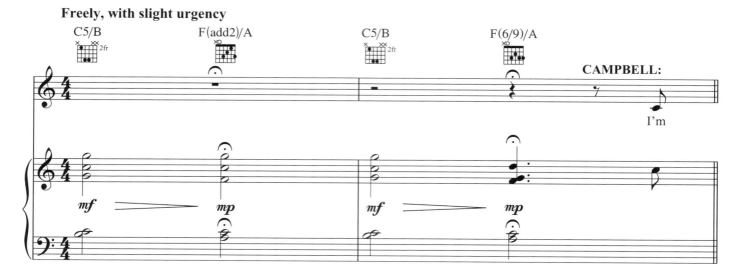

CAMPBELL:

I'm

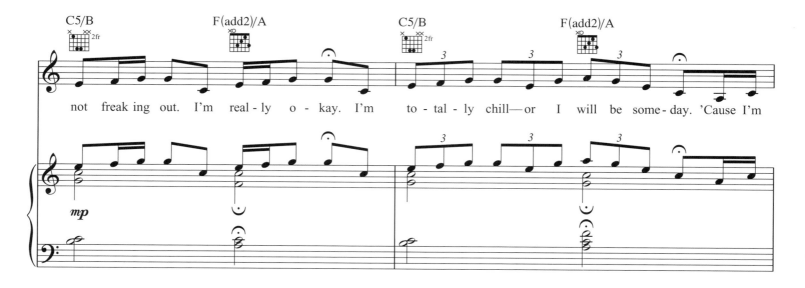

not freak ing out. I'm real-ly o-kay. I'm to-tal-ly chill—or I will be some-day. 'Cause I'm

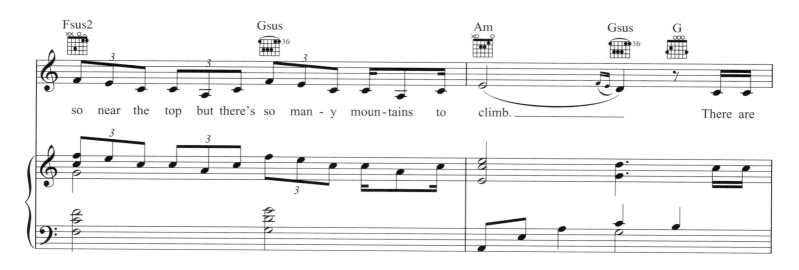

so near the top but there's so man-y moun-tains to climb. _____ There are

PINK
from WAR PAINT

Music by SCOTT FRANKEL
Lyrics by MICHAEL KORIE

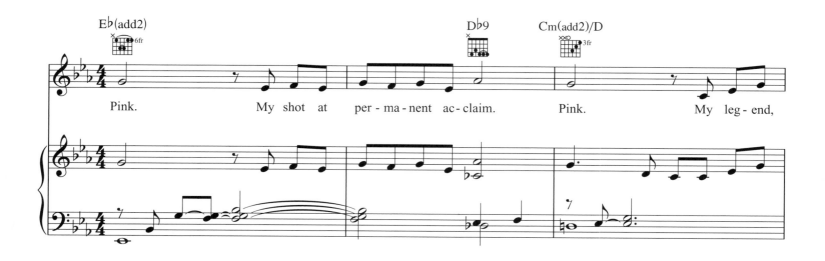

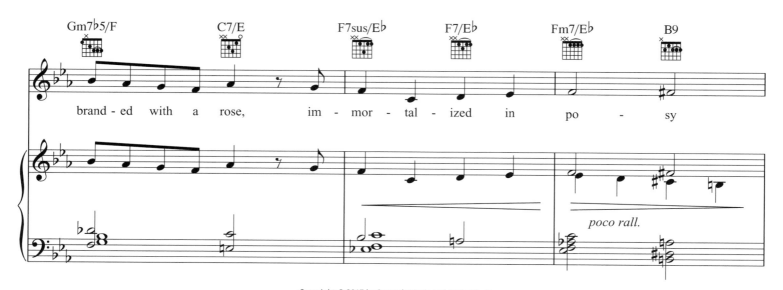

192

(reads the contract) *The undersigned hereby agrees to license her likeness and trademark color.*

(humming)

Mm

Very measured

a tempo e tranquillo

When I was just a farm girl in On-

tar - i - o, could an-y-one have known how far I'd

SANTA FE
from NEWSIES THE MUSICAL

Music by ALAN MENKEN
Lyrics by JACK FELDMAN

PROUD OF YOUR BOY

from ALADDIN

Music by ALAN MENKEN
Lyrics by HOWARD ASHMAN

PULLED
from THE ADDAMS FAMILY

Words and Music by
ANDREW LIPPA

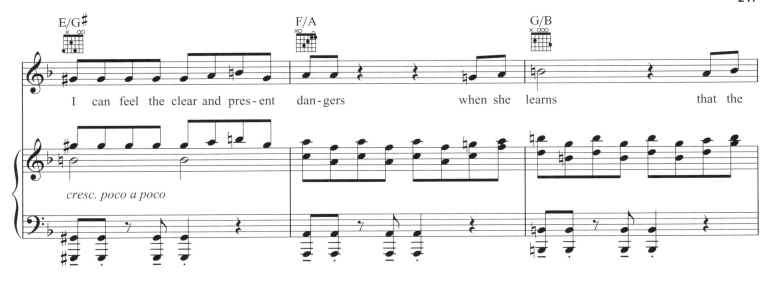

I can feel the clear and pres-ent dan-gers when she learns that the

boy _____ has got me pulled in a new di-rec-

tion, but I think I like ___ it. I think I like ___

PUGSLY:

Aaah! _

That was good, that was good.

(torture crank)

RIGHT HAND MAN

from SOMETHING ROTTEN!

Words and Music by WAYNE KIRKPATRICK
and KAREY KIRKPATRICK

SEE YOU LATER, ALLIGATOR

featured in the Broadway Musical MILLION DOLLAR QUARTET

Words and Music by
ROBERT GUIDRY

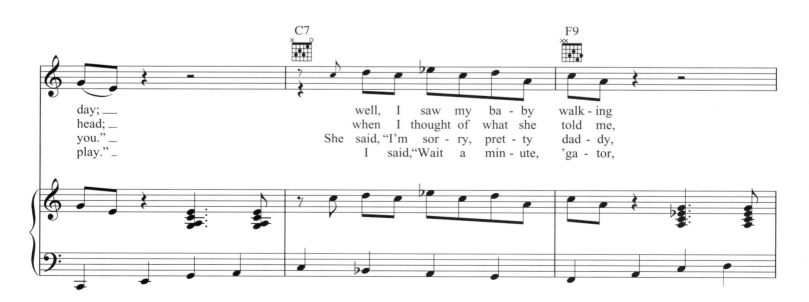

SOUL OF A MAN
from the Broadway Musical KINKY BOOTS

Words and Music by
CYNTHIA LAUPER

234

238

SHE USED TO BE MINE
from WAITRESS THE MUSICAL

Words and Music by
SARA BAREILLES

Moderately slow, in 1

It's not sim-ple to say _____ that most _ days _____ I don't rec-og-nize me that these shoes and this a-pron, that place and its pa-trons have tak-en more _____ than I gave _ them. _

STICK IT TO THE MAN

from SCHOOL OF ROCK

Music by ANDREW LLOYD WEBBER
Lyrics by GLENN SLATER

TESTIMONY
from AMAZING GRACE

Music and Lyrics by
CHRISTOPHER SMITH

Noble and energetic

WAVING THROUGH A WINDOW

from DEAR EVAN HANSEN

Music and Lyrics by BENJ PASEK
and JUSTIN PAUL

WHATEVER
from IT SHOULDA BEEN YOU

Words by BRIAN HARGROVE
Music by BARBARA ANSELMI

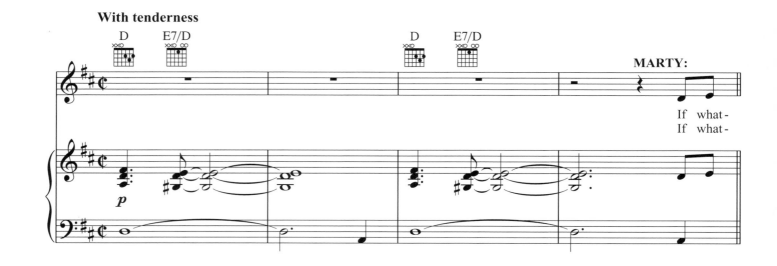

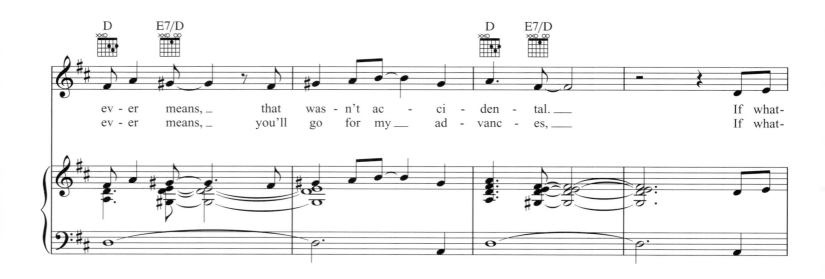

WHEN YOUR FEET DON'T TOUCH THE GROUND

from FINDING NEVERLAND

Words and Music by ELIOT KENNEDY
and GARY BARLOW

WHOA, MAMA

from BRIGHT STAR

Music by STEPHEN MARTIN
and EDIE BRICKELL
Lyrics by EDIE BRICKELL

You're a young girl _____ and you

ought-a know bet-ter than to be here.

What would ev-'ry-bod-y think?

YOU'LL BE BACK

from HAMILTON

Words and Music by
LIN-MANUEL MIRANDA

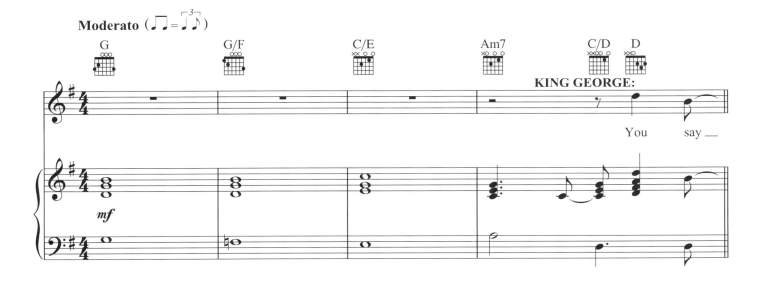

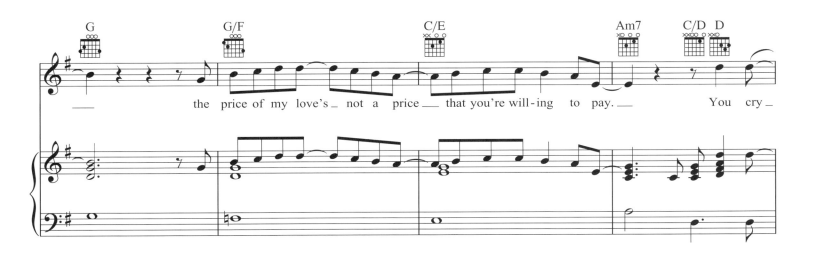

WITH YOU
from GHOST THE MUSICAL

Words and Music by GLEN BALLARD,
DAVID ALLAN STEWART and BRUCE JOEL RUBIN

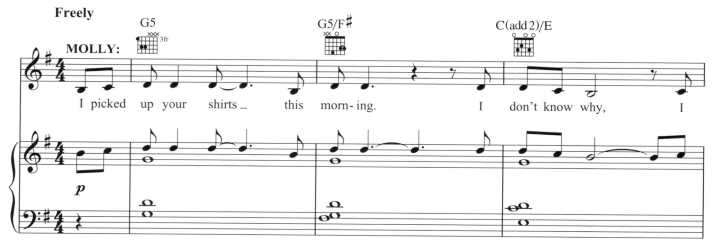

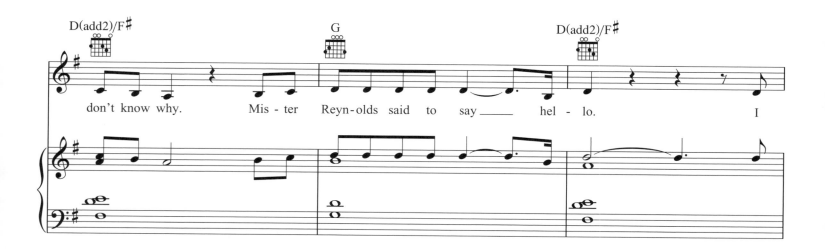

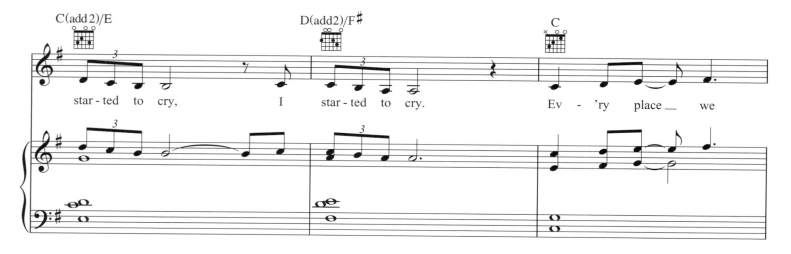

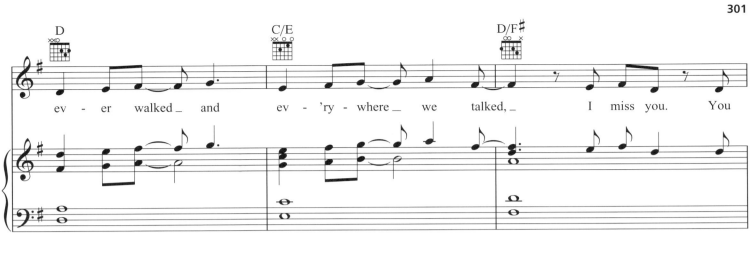

ev - er walked _ and ev - 'ry - where _ we talked, _ I miss you. You

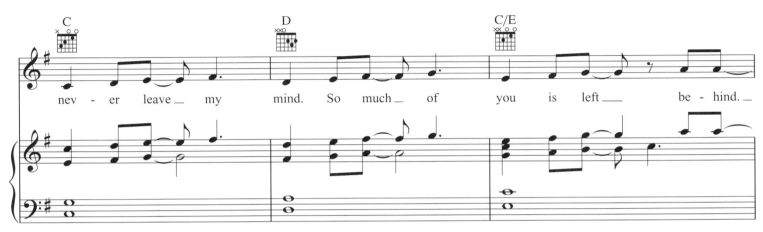

nev - er leave _ my mind. So much _ of you is left _ be - hind. _

Gentle Pop, a little faster

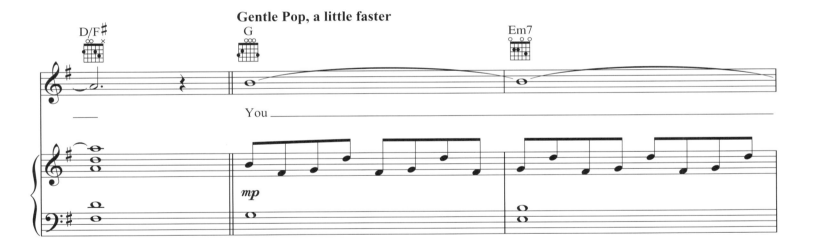

_ You _

took _ my days _ with you, _

307

YOU LEARN TO LIVE WITHOUT

from IF/THEN

Lyrics by BRIAN YORKEY
Music by TOM KITT

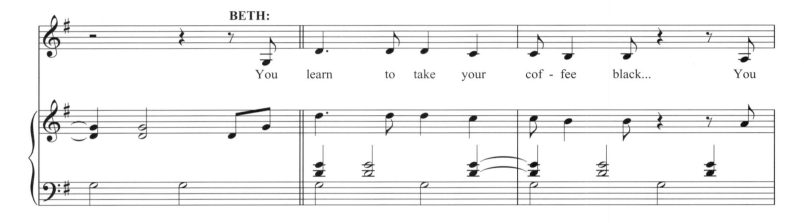

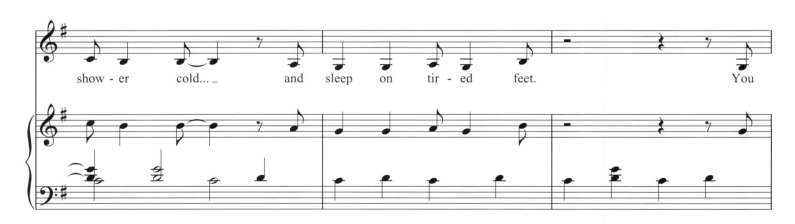

316

HAL LEONARD:
Your Source for the Best of Broadway

THE BEST BROADWAY SHEET MUSIC

A dazzling variety of songs are represented, including: Ain't Misbehavin' • Bewitched, Bothered, and Bewildered • Comedy Tonight • Don't Rain on My Parade • Everything's Coming Up Roses • Hopelessly Devoted to You • I Won't Grow Up • Lullaby of Broadway • On the Street Where You Live • Over the Rainbow • People • Ragtime • Suddenly, Seymour • Thank You for the Music • When I Look at You • and many more.

00322453 Piano/Vocal/Guitar $24.99

THE BEST BROADWAY SONGS EVER

Over 80 songs from Broadway's latest and greatest hit shows: As Long as He Needs Me • Bess, You Is My Woman • Bewitched • Comedy Tonight • Don't Cry for Me Argentina • Getting to Know You • I Could Have Danced All Night • I Dreamed a Dream • If I Were a Rich Man • The Last Night of the World • Love Changes Everything • Oklahoma • Ol' Man River • People • Try to Remember • and more.

00309155 Piano/Vocal/Guitar...................................$24.99

THE BEST SHOWTUNES EVER

This show-stopping collection features over 70 songs that'll make you want to sing and dance, including: Ain't Misbehavin' • Aquarius • But Not for Me • Day by Day • Defying Gravity • Forty-Second Street • It's De-Lovely • Lullaby of Broadway • On My Own • Over the Rainbow • Send in the Clowns • Singin' in the Rain • Summertime • Whatever Lola Wants (Lola Gets) • and more.

00118782 Piano/Vocal/Guitar...................................$19.99

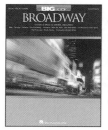

THE BIG BOOK OF BROADWAY

This edition includes 70 songs from classic musicals and recent blockbusters like *The Producers, Aida* and *Hairspray*. Includes: Bring Him Home • Camelot • Everything's Coming Up Roses • The Impossible Dream • A Lot of Livin' to Do • One • Some Enchanted Evening • Thoroughly Modern Millie • Till There Was You • and more.

00311658 Piano/Vocal/Guitar...................................$22.99

BROADWAY MUSICALS SHOW BY SHOW 2006-2013

31 shows are covered in the latest addition to this unique series, which showcases Broadway's biggest hits year-by-year and show-by-show. A sampling of the shows covered include: Spring Awakening (2006) • In the Heights (2008) • The Addams Family (2010) • The Book of Mormon (2011) • Once (2012) • A Gentleman's Guide to Love and Murder (2013) • and many more.

00123369 Piano/Vocal $19.99

BROADWAY SONGS

Get more bang for your buck with this jam-packed collection of 73 songs from 56 shows, including *Annie Get Your Gun, Cabaret, The Full Monty, Jekyll & Hyde, Les Misérables, Oklahoma* and more. Songs: Any Dream Will Do • Consider Yourself • Footloose • Getting to Know You • I Dreamed a Dream • One • People • Summer Nights • The Surrey with the Fringe on Top • With One Look • and more.

00310832 Piano/Vocal/Guitar...................................$14.99

DEFINITIVE BROADWAY

142 of the greatest show tunes ever, including: Don't Cry for Me Argentina • Hello, Dolly! • I Dreamed a Dream • Lullaby of Broadway • Mack the Knife • Memory • Send in the Clowns • Somewhere • The Sound of Music • Strike Up the Band • Summertime • Sunrise, Sunset • Tea for Two • Tomorrow • What I Did for Love • and more.

00359570 Piano/Vocal/Guitar $24.99

ESSENTIAL SONGS: BROADWAY

Over 100 songs are included in this top-notch collection: Any Dream Will Do • Blue Skies • Cabaret • Don't Cry for Me, Argentina • Edelweiss • Hello, Dolly! • I'll Be Seeing You • Memory • The Music of the Night • Oklahoma • Seasons of Love • Summer Nights • There's No Business like Show Business • Tomorrow • and more.

00311222 Piano/Vocal/Guitar..................................$24.99

FIRST 50 BROADWAY SONGS YOU SHOULD PLAY ON THE PIANO

50 simply arranged, must-know Broadway favorites are featured in this collection of easy piano arrangements. Includes: All I Ask of You • Cabaret • Consider Yourself • Don't Cry for Me Argentina • Edelweiss • Getting to Know You • Hello, Dolly! • I Could Have Danced All Night • I Dreamed a Dream • Memory • Oh, What a Beautiful Mornin' • Ol' Man River • Sunrise, Sunset • Tomorrow • and more.

00150167 Easy Piano $14.99

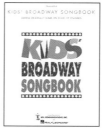

KIDS' BROADWAY SONGBOOK

An unprecedented collection of songs originally performed by children on the Broadway stage. Includes 16 songs for boys and girls, including: Gary, Indiana (*The Music Man*) • Castle on a Cloud (*Les Misérables*) • Where Is Love? (*Oliver!*) • Tomorrow (*Annie*) • and more.

00311609 Book Only $16.99
00740149 Book/Online Audio $24.99

THE OFF-BROADWAY SONGBOOK

42 gems from off-Broadway hits, including *Godspell, Tick Tick... Boom!, The Fantasticks, Once upon a Mattress, The Wild Party* and more. Songs include: Always a Bridesmaid • Come to Your Senses • Day by Day • Happiness • How Glory Goes • I Hate Musicals • The Picture in the Hall • Soon It's Gonna Rain • Stars and the Moon • Still Hurting • Twilight • and more.

00311168 Piano/Vocal/Guitar..................................$19.99

THE TONY AWARDS SONGBOOK

This collection assembles songs from each of Tony-winning Best Musicals through "Mama Who Bore Me" from 2007 winner *Spring Awakening*. Songs include: Til There Was You • The Sound of Music • Hello, Dolly! • Sunrise, Sunset • Send in the Clowns • Tomorrow • Memory • I Dreamed a Dream • Seasons of Love • Circle of Life • Mama, I'm a Big Girl Now • and more. Includes photos and a table of contents listed both chronologically and alphabetically.

00311092 Piano/Vocal/Guitar..................................$19.95

Prices, contents, and availability subject to change without notice.
Some products may not be available outside the U.S.A.

Get complete songlists and more at **www.halleonard.com**

1217

CLASSIC COLLECTIONS OF YOUR FAVORITE SONGS

arranged for piano, voice, and guitar

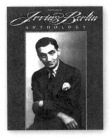

Irving Berlin Anthology

A comprehensive collection of 61 timeless songs with a bio, song background notes, and photos. Songs include: Always • Blue Skies • Cheek to Cheek • God Bless America • Marie • Puttin' on the Ritz • Steppin' Out with My Baby • There's No Business Like Show Business • White Christmas • (I Wonder Why?) You're Just in Love • and more.

00312493... $22.99

The Big Book of Standards

86 classics essential to any music library, including: April in Paris • Autumn in New York • Blue Skies • Cheek to Cheek • Heart and Soul • I Left My Heart in San Francisco • In the Mood • Isn't It Romantic? • Mona Lisa • Moon River • The Nearness of You • Out of Nowhere • Spanish Eyes • Star Dust • Stella by Starlight • That Old Black Magic • They Say It's Wonderful • What Now My Love • and more.

00311667.............. $19.95

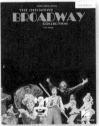

The Definitive Broadway Collection – Second Edition

142 of the greatest show tunes compiled into one volume! Songs include: Don't Cry for Me Argentina • Edelweiss • Hello, Dolly! • I Could Have Danced All Night • I Dreamed a Dream • I Know Him So Well • Lullabye of Broadway • Mack the Knife • People • Send in the Clowns • Somewhere • Summertime • Sunrise, Sunset • Tomorrow • more.

00359570 .... $27.50

The Great American Songbook – The Composers

From Berlin to Gershwin to Carmichael to Cahn, this folio features a comprehensive collection of standards from the greatest American composers. Includes beloved standards such as: Ain't Misbehavin' • Cheek to Cheek • Don't Get Around Much Anymore • Moon River • and dozens more.

00311365.............................. $24.99

The Great American Songbook – The Singers

Crooners, wailers, shouters, balladeers: some of our greatest pop vocalists have poured their hearts and souls into the musical gems of the Great American Songbook. This folio features 100 of these classics by Louis Armstrong, Tony Bennett, Rosemary Clooney, Nat "King" Cole, Bing Crosby, Doris Day, Ella Fitzgerald, Judy Garland, Dean Martin, Frank Sinatra, Barbra Streisand, Mel Tormé, and others.

00311433 .... $24.95

I'll Be Seeing You! – 2nd Edition

A salute to the music and memories of WWII, including a year-by-year chronology of events on the homefront, dozens of photos, and 50 radio favorites of the GIs and their families back home, including: Boogie Woogie Bugle Boy • Don't Sit Under the Apple Tree (With Anyone Else But Me) • I Don't Want to Walk Without You • I'll Be Seeing You • Moonlight in Vermont • There's a Star-Spangled Banner Waving Somewhere • You'd Be So Nice to Come Home To • and more.

00311698............................. $19.95

Lounge Music – 2nd Edition

Features over 50 top requests of the martini crowd: All the Way • Fever • I Write the Songs • Misty • Moon River • That's Amore (That's Love) • Yesterday • more.

00310193 .... $15.95

The Henry Mancini Collection

This superb collection includes 45 songs spanning Mancini's illustrious career: Baby Elephant Walk • Breakfast at Tiffany's • Charade • Days of Wine and Roses • Mr. Lucky • Moon River • Peter Gunn • The Pink Panther • A Shot in the Dark • The Thorn Birds • and more.

00313522 .... $19.99

Ladies of Song

This terrific collection includes over 70 songs associated with some of the greatest female vocalists ever recorded. Songs include: Cabaret • Downtown • The First Time Ever I Saw Your Face • God Bless' the Child • If I Were a Bell • My Funny Valentine • One for My Baby (And One More for the Road) • The Way We Were • and many more.

00311948... $19.95

The Best of Rodgers & Hammerstein

A capsule of 26 classics from this legendary duo. Songs include: Climb Ev'ry Mountain • Edelweiss • Getting to Know You • I'm Gonna Wash That Man Right Outta My Hair • My Favorite Things • Oklahoma • The Surrey with the Fringe on Top • You'll Never Walk Alone • and more.

00308210................................... $16.95

The Best Songs Ever – 9th Edition

One of the bestselling songbooks of all time, now updated to a 9th edition! Includes 71 all-time hits, including: Always • Bohemian Rhapsody • Every Breath You Take • Fly Me to the Moon (In Other Words) • Hallelujah • Happy • Love Me Tender • Memory • My Favorite Things • Over the Rainbow • Piano Man • Unforgettable • Yesterday • You Raise Me Up • and many more.

00265721 .... $24.99

Torch Songs – 2nd Edition

Sing your heart out with this collection of 59 sultry jazz and big band melancholy masterpieces, including: Angel Eyes • Cry Me a River • I Can't Get Started • I Got It Bad and That Ain't Good • I'm Glad There Is You • Lover Man (Oh, Where Can You Be?) • Misty • My Funny Valentine • Stormy Weather • and many more! 224 pages.

00490446............................. $17.99

www.halleonard.com

BIG BOOKS of Music

Our "Big Books" feature big selections of popular titles under one cover, perfect for performing musicians, music aficionados or the serious hobbyist. All books are arranged for piano, voice, and guitar, and feature stay-open binding, so the books lie flat without breaking the spine.

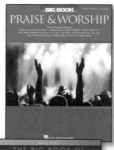

BIG BOOK OF BALLADS – 2ND ED.
62 songs.
00310485 .... $19.95

BIG BOOK OF BIG BAND HITS
84 songs.
00310701 .... $22.99

BIG BOOK OF BLUEGRASS SONGS
70 songs.
00311484 .... $19.95

BIG BOOK OF BLUES
80 songs.
00311843 .... $19.99

BIG BOOK OF BROADWAY
70 songs.
00311658 .... $22.99

BIG BOOK OF CHILDREN'S SONGS
55 songs.
00359261 .... $16.99

GREAT BIG BOOK OF CHILDREN'S SONGS
76 songs.
00310002 .... $15.99

BIG BOOK OF CHRISTMAS SONGS – 2ND ED.
126 songs.
00311520 .... $19.95

BIG BOOK OF CLASSICAL MUSIC
100 songs.
00310508 .... $19.99

BIG BOOK OF CONTEMPORARY CHRISTIAN FAVORITES – 3RD ED.
50 songs.
00312067 .... $21.99

BIG BOOK OF FOLKSONGS
125 songs.
00312549 .... $19.99

BIG BOOK OF FRENCH SONGS
70 songs.
00311154 .... $22.99

BIG BOOK OF GERMAN SONGS
78 songs.
00311816 .... $19.99

BIG BOOK OF GOSPEL SONGS
100 songs.
00310604 .... $19.95

BIG BOOK OF HYMNS
125 hymns.
00310510 .... $19.99

BIG BOOK OF IRISH SONGS
76 songs.
00310981 .... $19.99

BIG BOOK OF ITALIAN FAVORITES
80 songs.
00311185 .... $19.99

BIG BOOK OF JAZZ – 2ND ED.
75 songs.
00311557 .... $22.99

BIG BOOK OF LATIN AMERICAN SONGS
89 songs.
00311562 .... $19.95

BIG BOOK OF LOVE SONGS – 3RD. ED.
82 songs.
00257807 .... $22.99

BIG BOOK OF MOTOWN
84 songs.
00311061 .... $19.95

BIG BOOK OF NOSTALGIA
158 songs.
00310004 .... $24.99

BIG BOOK OF OLDIES
73 songs.
00310756 .... $19.95

THE BIG BOOK OF PRAISE & WORSHIP
52 songs.
00140795 .... $22.99

BIG BOOK OF RAGTIME PIANO
63 songs.
00311749 .... $19.95

BIG BOOK OF STANDARDS
86 songs.
00311667 .... $19.95

BIG BOOK OF SWING
84 songs.
00310359 .... $19.95

BIG BOOK OF TORCH SONGS – 2ND ED.
75 songs.
00310561 .... $19.99

BIG BOOK OF TV THEME SONGS
78 songs.
00310504 .... $19.95

BIG BOOK OF WEDDING MUSIC
77 songs.
00311567 .... $22.99

Visit **www.halleonard.com**
for our entire catalog and to view our complete songlists.